D1416600

A Medieval Castle

Other titles in the Great Structures in History
series include:

The Great Wall of China
The Panama Canal
The Roman Colosseum
Stonehenge

A Medieval Castle

GREAT STRUCTURES IN HISTORY

Gail Jarrow

KIDHAVEN PRESS

An imprint of Thomson Gale, a part of The Thomson Corporation

THOMSON

GALE

Detroit • New York • San Francisco • San Diego • New Haven, Conn.
Waterville, Maine • London • Munich

For more information, contact
KidHaven Press
27500 Drake Rd.
Farmington Hills, MI 48331-3535
Or you can visit our Internet site at http://www.gale.com

LIBRARY OF CONGRESS CATALOGING-IN-PUBLICATION DATA

Jarrow, Gail, 1952-
  A Medieval Castle / by Gail Jarrow.
    p. cm. -- (Great structures in history)
  Includes bibliographical references.
Summary: Discusses medieval castles: why they were built, who built them, how they were constructed, how they were used, their deterioration, and their repair and restoration.
  ISBN 0-7377-2070-0
  1. Medieval castle--History--Juvenile Literature. [Medieval castles--History.]
I. Title. II. Series.

Contents

CHAPTER ONE 6
The Castle—a Fortified House

CHAPTER TWO 14
Building the Castle

CHAPTER THREE 23
Defending Against Attack

CHAPTER FOUR 31
Castles Under Siege

Glossary 41

For Further Reading 43

Index 45

Picture Credits 47

About the Author 48

The Castle—a Fortified House

The massive stone towers, thick walls, moats, and drawbridges of castles are left over from the time of **medieval** kings and knights. Medieval times, also known as the **Middle Ages**, is what historians call the period from about A.D. 500 to 1500.

Many castles were built during the last half of the Middle Ages. Historians believe that between seventy-five thousand and one hundred thousand castles were erected in Europe from the tenth through fifteenth centuries. They refer to this time as the age of castles. Castles were used as homes, **fortresses**, and government buildings, and they were an important part of medieval life.

Sign of Power and Wealth

In medieval society, people who controlled the land had the most power and wealth. Landowners built castles to show off their power and to discourage enemies from attacking. The most powerful landowners built several castles throughout their vast estates.

Kings gave land to **nobles** so that the nobles would swear **allegiance** and promise to defend the king, his castle, and his lands. The nobles then built their own castles on the land they had been given.

More than seventy-five thousand castles were built in Europe during the Middle Ages.

The castle served as a home for the noble (also called a lord), his family, and his servants. From the castle, the lord of the manor ruled over his land and the people living on it. Peasant farmers and villagers paid rents, taxes, and a portion of their crops to the lord. In return, the lord allowed the peasants to live and work on his manor. To defend his home and property from enemies, the lord recruited knights. The castle was the knights' base.

Local government was conducted from the castle. Often the castle was the center of business where farmers,

The castle family ate their meals and entertained guests in the great hall, the main room of the castle.

traders, and craftspeople sold their wares. In certain areas, towns grew up next to castles. In other places, the town or village was part of the castle grounds and was surrounded by a protective wall.

The Comforts of Home

Since a castle was the home of a wealthy lord, it was built to provide as much comfort as possible. The lord and his family lived in the safest part of the castle. In early castles, this was in a cramped tower. Later castles had larger living quarters, including a great hall, which was the castle's main room.

Castle residents ate meals and entertained visitors in the great hall. The lord and his family slept in an area separated from the hall by curtains. Everyone else slept on the hall's floor or benches. As castles became larger and fancier over time, sleeping chambers for the lord's family were moved to an upper story.

Most castles had a chapel where castle residents worshipped. This could be a small room within the tower or a separate building on the castle grounds. In large castles, the lord and his family had their own private chapel within their living quarters. A second chapel was set aside for servants, knights, and other residents of the castle.

Smoky, Drafty, and Dark

In the early castles, heat came from a smoky open fire in the center of the great hall. Eventually castle builders installed fireplaces with vents called flues to direct smoke out of the building. Castles, however, were still drafty. Window openings usually did not have glass, but they could be closed with wooden shutters. Wall hangings and tapestries covered walls to provide decoration and insulation from the cold.

Little daylight entered a castle because the window openings were narrow and the walls were thick. Candles and torches provided light, even during the day.

Castles were built to give a clear view of approaching invaders and to provide protection for the king, his family, and supporters.

Castles had toilets, although they were crude by modern standards. The toilet, called a **garderobe,** was a seat built into an outside stone wall. Wastes fell down a chute into a ditch, moat, or river. In some castles, the garderobe drained into a hole in the tower's basement.

A Fortified Home

Competition for land and power led to warfare among rival kings and nobles. The lord's castle was designed to protect him during dangerous times. If an attack looked likely, the lord also allowed people living on his land to come inside the castle walls for protection. The word *castle* hints at the structure's connection to military defense. It comes from *castellum*, the name Romans called their forts.

Castles were key to a king's authority. Kings built castle strongholds across their kingdoms to maintain their power. When a king and his supporters conquered new land, the king erected a castle and supplied it with knights to enforce his rule.

Castles were often used to protect borders. For example, the English kings built castles along their borders with Scotland and Wales to keep these neighbors in check. In parts of Europe, castles were used to defend against foreign invaders, such as the Mongols and Arabs.

When a medieval king traveled, he and his attendants stayed at his castles or at castles built by friendly nobles. Several twelfth-century English kings spent more money on castle building than on any other single item in their budgets.

Picking the Perfect Site

Castle builders frequently chose a location with a military advantage. They placed castles along travel routes such as rivers, mountain passes, ports, and key roads. Enemies using these routes were forced to go by the castle, and their approach was spotted from the castle. An armed force could be sent out to check on the strangers and, if necessary, beat back an attack.

A castle built on a mountain or high hill gave defenders a clear view of advancing invaders in the valley or valleys below. In addition, the high ground was difficult to attack. Many castles in Spain, Italy, Germany, France, and Wales were built on steep hills or rocky outcrops that were nearly impossible for attackers to climb.

Building a castle near water was another way to protect it from invaders. If a castle was surrounded by marshes, it could not be attacked by heavy weapons, because they

Castles were often built in high places or near water to make them easier to defend against enemies.

would sink into the soggy ground. Castles built on islands were easy to defend because they could be approached only by boat or over a well-guarded bridge or causeway. When an island site could not be found, some castle builders dammed streams or rivers to form an artificial lake around the castle.

Different Styles

Medieval castles had different features depending on the time period and where they were built. Early timber castles could be constructed in a few weeks. Stone castles took years to finish. Some castles were located in cities, and others were built in rural areas. All were designed to keep out enemies.

CHAPTER TWO

Building the Castle

When nobles built their castles, they used many of the defensive features found in ancient military fortresses. Whether made of wood or stone, medieval castles shared the same basic design—a safe, secure tower and a protective wall surrounding the castle grounds.

Motte and Bailey Castles

Wooden castles were popular at the beginning of the age of castles—from the tenth through twelfth centuries. A wooden tower sat atop a hill, called the **motte**. The area around the bottom of the motte was used as a courtyard, or **bailey**. A timber wall surrounded the bailey.

Hundreds of motte and bailey castles were built during this period—especially in England and France. A motte and bailey castle could be built cheaply and quickly. The dirt and wood building materials were easy to find in forested areas. Local, unskilled workers could erect a motte and bailey castle within a few weeks.

Builders first piled up dirt and stone to form the motte, which means "mound of earth." In some places, the mound was a natural hill that castle builders cut away in order to form a steep slope. Motte heights ranged from 10 feet (3 meters) to almost 100 feet (30.5 meters).

A deep ditch surrounded the base of the motte. Dirt dug from the ditch was used to build up the mound. The ditch, which frequently contained water, was too wide for attackers to cross easily. Over time, this ditch became known as a **moat**, from the word *motte*.

Safe Living Quarters

The wooden tower on the top of the motte became the living quarters for the lord and his family. It was called a **keep** because the lord was "kept" there. The keep included space for eating, sleeping, and storing supplies and weapons.

Most keeps were rectangular or square, not rounded. Tower sizes varied from one to three stories. The combined height of the motte and keep was tall enough for castle residents to spot approaching enemies.

The keep entrance was usually above ground level. The only way in was by ladder or removable bridge. These could be pulled up or destroyed during an attack. The keep

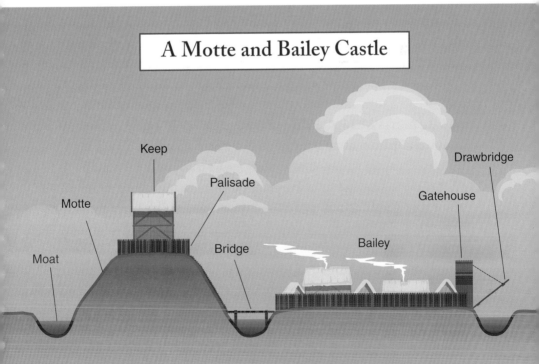

A Motte and Bailey Castle

Keep

Palisade

Drawbridge

Motte

Gatehouse

Moat

Bridge

Bailey

was the safest part of the castle, and castle residents retreated there when the enemy attacked.

The Palisade and Bailey

A tall wooden fence called a **palisade** surrounded the top of the motte and provided extra security for the keep. A second palisade and ditch enclosed the bailey. The entrance into the bailey was guarded by a wooden **gatehouse**. From the gatehouse, defenders could raise the wooden **drawbridge** that rested over the ditch and prevent attackers from entering the castle.

The bailey was large enough to hold stables, storehouses, kitchens, and wooden huts for servants and craftspeople, such as bakers and blacksmiths. In many castles, this courtyard also had gardens, grazing space for animals, and room for knights to train.

In some motte and bailey castles, the bailey surrounded the entire base of the motte. In others, it only extended from one side of the hill in a semicircle. A castle could have several baileys, each surrounded by its own ditch and palisade. The bailey closest to the motte housed the lord's servants. The next one was for craftspeople, and the farthest from the keep was for peasants who worked the lord's fields.

The Disadvantages of Wood

Although motte and bailey castles were inexpensive and quickly built, they had disadvantages. The wood eventually rotted and had to be replaced. Wooden walls were more vulnerable in an attack because towers and palisades could be burned. A burning wooden castle is pictured in the **Bayeux Tapestry**, an eleventh-century wall hanging. It shows soldiers setting fire to a castle palisade at Dinan in France and forcing the noble inside to surrender.

The wealthier nobles started replacing the wooden motte and bailey castles with stone, a stronger and more

Both wood and stone castles shared the same basic design, including courtyards with gardens.

permanent material. The change from wood to stone happened over many years. Less wealthy nobles continued to build wooden motte and bailey castles until the end of the thirteenth century.

The Switch to Stone

New stone castles were often built on the sites of old motte and bailey castles using the same mounds, ditches, and layout. The wooden keep on top of the motte, however, was replaced with stone, which provided more protection.

Stone keeps, like wooden ones, were usually square or rectangular. The keep's walls were thick and had small window openings, making the keep easier to defend than the wooden tower had been. The building had no ground-level

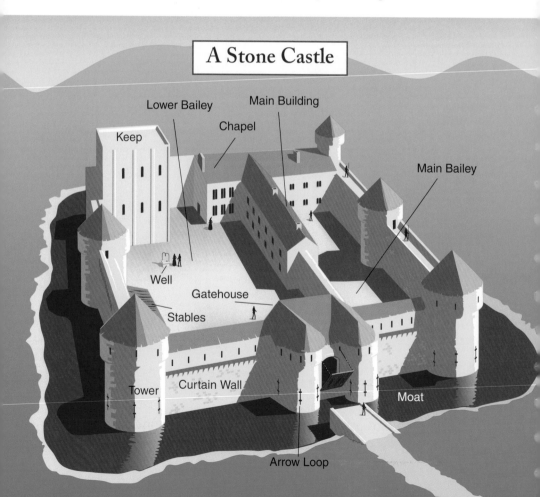

A Stone Castle

Lower Bailey
Main Building
Chapel
Keep
Main Bailey
Well
Gatehouse
Stables
Tower
Curtain Wall
Moat
Arrow Loop

entrance, and the stairs to the second-story entrance could be removed during an attack to keep the enemy out.

If the attackers still managed to get inside, the defenders made use of a narrow spiral staircase to help fight them off. The spiral staircase usually turned clockwise as it rose. This allowed a defender holding a sword in his right hand to fight an attacker coming up the staircase toward him. The attacker, however, had to lead with his left side as he climbed the stairs. This made it awkward for him to fight with his right hand.

Stone Walls

A stone keep protected those inside it, but castle builders wanted even more security. They eventually replaced the wooden palisades of the motte and bailey castle with a stone wall called a **curtain wall**. The wall provided the main defense of the castle.

Curtain walls were at least 15 to 35 feet (4.6 to 10.7 meters) high so that enemies could not easily climb over them. They were at least 6 to 9 feet (1.8 to 2.7 meters) thick, and often much thicker. Such strong walls could resist attack better than the wooden palisades. **Wall walks** along the top of the curtain gave defenders room to move around as they fought off invaders.

With strong curtain walls protecting the bailey, the lord's quarters could be safely moved from the keep to roomier living space in the bailey. By the second half of the thirteenth century, many new castles did not have a separate keep. Instead the lord's private rooms were built against the walls of the thick, protective curtain.

Building a Stone Castle

Castles with tall towers and thick walls were difficult to build. The construction of a large stone castle was an expensive and long process requiring at least one thousand

Stone keeps were usually square or rectangular and were the safest part of the castle.

workers. Once a noble decided to build a stone castle, he hired a master builder to find the best location, to design the structure, and to oversee construction.

Diggers collected the stone and hauled it to the building site in carts. Stoneworkers, called **masons**, cut and carved the stone into blocks using axes and chisels. Workers lifted the stone blocks with pulleys and wooden ramps. Then the masons laid the blocks into proper position on the castle walls.

Other workers mixed mortar from lime, sand, and water to cement the stone blocks together. Carpenters built floors, doors, and ceiling beams. Smiths made the metal parts of the castle such as nails, locks, hinges, and iron grates. Ditchdiggers dug the moat around the castle. In some locations, this meant cutting into solid rock.

Collecting, cutting, moving, and laying the stone was slow, hard work. Construction stopped in winter because wet mortar cracked in cold temperatures. As a result, it could take a year to add 10 to 12 feet (3 to 3.7 meters) to the height of a stone keep. Finishing an entire castle could

It could take a year to add ten to twelve feet to a castle wall because collecting, cutting, moving, and laying the stone was such slow, hard work.

It usually took at least a thousand workers five years or more to build a stone castle.

take five years or longer. One castle in Wales took more than twenty-five years to build.

Changes Continued

Castle design continued to change throughout the Middle Ages. Builders found better ways to protect the residents from attackers. These improvements were included as new castles were built and were often added to older castles.

CHAPTER THREE

Defending Against Attack

As time passed, armies developed more damaging weapons and new ways to attack castles. To resist the enemy, defenders strengthened the castle's defenses.

Preparing for a Siege

An important part of castle defense was withstanding a **siege**—when attackers blocked delivery of food and drinking water. Many castle builders built storage areas that could hold enough food to last many months. If defenders knew that an attack was coming, they brought in additional fresh food.

Defenders also planned for sieges by digging protected wells within the walls. Despite good planning, however, some wells went dry because too many people took refuge inside the castle and used up all of the water. Attackers sometimes set fire to wooden buildings inside the castle by throwing burning objects over the wall. Then defenders had to use their limited water to put out the flames. When the drinking water ran out, the castle residents had to surrender.

Walls for Defense

In addition to cutting off food and water, attackers used force to take control of a castle. They bombarded walls with huge boulders or hurled rocks over the curtain wall.

As extra protection, some castles were built with an inside curtain wall that was higher than the outside one.

To provide better defense against these attacks, builders made walls thicker and higher.

Some castles were designed with two or more curtain walls. The extra curtains made it harder for attackers to break into a castle. The inner curtain was higher than the outer one. Arrow-shooting defenders, called **archers**, standing on top of the inner curtain could shoot at the enemy outside the castle over the heads of defenders on the outer curtain. Even if attackers managed to take control of the outer curtain and break into the castle grounds, they became easy targets for archers on the inner curtain.

To prevent the enemy from breaking through the bottom of a curtain wall, castle builders thickened the base with stone or mounded dirt. The slope formed by the extra stone or dirt stopped attackers from placing ladders directly against the wall. In addition, rocks dropped from the top of the wall by defenders were deflected by the slope and hit the enemy.

Top of the Wall

Defenders on top of the walls were protected by a toothlike barrier on the outer edge of the wall walk. This barrier, called a **battlement**, had open sections called **crenels** where defenders stood to shoot arrows at approaching attackers. The alternating high stone sections, called **merlons**, shielded the wall walk from enemy arrows.

Many castles also had a feature that allowed defenders to see the enemy directly below without leaning over the battlement. A wooden platform called a **hoarding** extended from the edge of the battlement over the ground. The hoarding contained holes through which defenders

The top of the castle wall was protected by the battlement where archers could shoot arrows at invaders.

dropped heavy objects or hot liquids on attackers. A roof protected the defenders from attackers' arrows and rocks. Wet animal hides covered the hoarding roof to resist fire from attackers' flaming arrows.

Wooden hoardings were temporary; they were put in place when an attack was expected. Some castle builders later replaced wood hoardings with permanent stone structures that did not burn.

Keeping Attackers Away

Defenders used barriers to prevent attackers from getting close to the castle walls. Thorny hedges protected the base from climbers and diggers. Moats around the walls were up to 60 feet (18.3 meters) wide and 30 feet (9.1 meters) deep. Dry moats often contained sharpened stakes on the bottom and sides to discourage the enemy from approaching. A water-filled moat stopped attackers from filling in the ditch with dirt or brush or from tunneling under the wall.

Defenders cleared trees and brush from a wide area around the castle to prevent the enemy from sneaking up on them. During a siege, the cleared land allowed the defenders to watch the attackers' movements and to prepare for attacks on the walls.

Protecting the Entrance

Because of barriers and wall defenses, the curtain wall was hard to attack. The castle's weak spot was its entrance. A gatehouse protected the doorway in the curtain. Unlike the simple, wooden gatehouse of a motte and bailey castle, the gatehouse of a stone castle was a fortified building that guarded the entrance using bridges, heavy gates, traps, and obstacles. Some gatehouses were so heavily protected that their upper floors were used for living quarters.

In some castles, the gatehouse was a single tower built along the curtain wall with the castle's entrance on its

The gatehouse, traps, bridges, thorny hedges, and moats protected the entrance of the castle.

ground level. In other castles, the entrance was placed between two stone towers, each two or three stories high. The entrance was about 6 feet wide (1.8 meters), only room enough for a horse and cart to pass through.

Defenders in the gatehouse controlled a wooden drawbridge across the moat. When the drawbridge was raised, enemies could not get near the castle entrance. A wooden gate strengthened with iron, called a **portcullis**, moved up and down in the walls of the gatehouse. It could be lowered more quickly than the drawbridge could be raised. Some castles had more than one portcullis. If the enemy got inside the entry, both gates were dropped. This trapped

A Counterweight Drawbridge

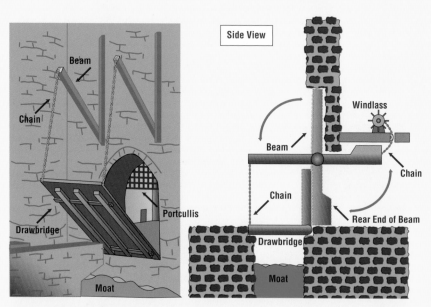

Some castle drawbridges operated using counterweights. The drawbridge usually rested over the moat. To raise the bridge, defenders allowed the heavy rear ends of large beams to fall. As the lighter front ends rose, the chains raised the bridge.

the invaders in between the gates where defenders could easily attack them.

A narrow passage led from the entrance through the gatehouse into the castle grounds. The passage had obstacles to hinder invaders, such as sharp turns or hidden pits. The ceiling above the passage contained openings that were called **murder holes**. Defenders used murder holes to shoot arrows and drop rocks, boiling water, or hot sand onto intruders. If the enemy lit a fire in the entrance, defenders poured water through the murder holes onto the flames.

Improving the Towers

In addition to the gatehouse towers, builders added towers along the curtain wall. These towers stuck out from the curtain and rose higher than it. Archers could stand on top of the towers and shoot at invaders who climbed the walls or ran along the wall walks.

The corners of square and rectangular towers and keeps, however, proved to be a weakness. In several successful sieges of the early thirteenth century, attackers hammered at tower corners with hurled boulders or wooden beams. When the stone gave way, the invaders broke in and took control of the castle. Attackers could also tunnel under a corner of a rectangular tower and weaken its foundation until the tower collapsed.

Castle designers realized that curved walls without corners could stand up better against the usual attack methods. They built rounded towers to help defenders battle invaders. Without corners cutting off their view, defenders could see more of the curtain wall and ground.

Inside the Tower

To strengthen the tower's defenses, castle builders added wall openings called **arrow loops**. On the inside, an arrow loop was wide enough for archers to shoot out. On the

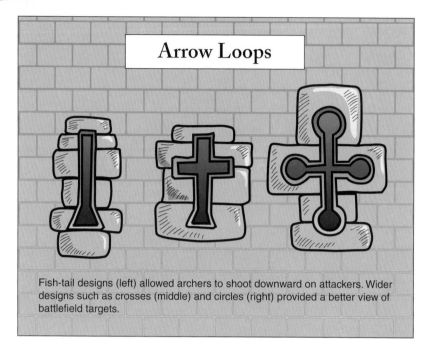

Arrow Loops

Fish-tail designs (left) allowed archers to shoot downward on attackers. Wider designs such as crosses (middle) and circles (right) provided a better view of battlefield targets.

outside, however, it was too narrow for attackers to shoot into. Arrow loops were placed so that the entire curtain wall and land around the castle were within the archers' shooting range.

The doors into the towers were constructed with oak planks, metal plates, and heavy nails. They could be locked from the inside with a beam. Since doorways were only wide enough for one person, they were easier to defend. With small window openings and strong doors, towers were difficult to invade.

Built for Strength

A castle was designed to withstand battering and to drive back the enemy. Because of its many protective features, a castle could be defended against an army of attackers.

CHAPTER FOUR

Castles Under Siege

Defenders inside a strong castle usually refused to surrender to their enemy. But attackers had several ways to overcome this resistance. These methods included trickery, siege, and special weapons that could destroy the castle.

Trickery

When attackers planned to use the castle themselves, they did not want to destroy it. Instead, they tried to take control through trickery. Sometimes traitors inside the castle smuggled attackers inside or opened the gates for them. Other times clever invaders sneaked into the castle, perhaps hidden in a wagon or disguised as visitors. Once inside, they opened the gate for their fellow attackers before the defenders realized what had happened.

Trickery brought down the Chateau Gaillard, a castle that many said could never be taken. England's King Richard the Lion-Hearted built it on steep cliffs in France at the end of the twelfth century. The castle had strong defenses, including three curtain walls.

In 1203 the French king set out to take the castle from the English. His army had been unable to overcome the castle's defenses until someone spotted an unguarded

The French attacked King Richard the Lion-Hearted and his Chateau Gaillard (pictured here) by sneaking in through an unguarded garderobe.

garderobe chute on a curtain wall. Without being seen by the defenders, a small group of attackers crawled up the chute. They sneaked into the castle's middle bailey through an unlocked window in the castle's chapel. Once inside, the invaders lowered the drawbridge over the moat, and the French charged into the bailey. Eventually, with no hope of escape, the English defenders surrendered.

Under Siege

When attackers could not invade the castle through trickery, they put the castle under siege by cutting it off from the outside. The trapped defenders sometimes surrendered in return for their safe release. But if defenders had ample food, water, and weapons, they often refused to give up.

To force surrender, the attackers made life unbearable within the castle. For example, they hurled diseased animals over the castle walls to sicken the people inside. If the castle's water supply came from an outside spring, the attackers poisoned the water. Still, defenders often held out for many months, even years, hoping that friends would arrive to help them.

Assault on the Castle

The waiting attackers frequently became impatient. Soldiers grew tired of camping in harsh weather. Sometimes they ran out of food or became ill. The attackers did not want to fight a rescuing army. Instead they decided to take the castle by launching an assault.

Attackers broke through the walls, climbed over them, and made them collapse. An assault either frightened the defenders into surrender or allowed the attackers to get inside the castle.

Breaking In

To break through walls, doors, and gates, attackers used an iron-tipped **battering ram**, a heavy wooden beam made from a tree trunk. A dozen or more soldiers swung it back and forth against the target until the stone or wood gave way.

Defenders on the wall shot arrows or threw stones and boiling liquids down at the soldiers. To shield themselves, the men worked under a portable wooden shelter. The shelter usually had wheels for easy movement and was covered with animal hides to resist fire.

Climbing Over

While soldiers pounded the castle with battering rams,

Attackers used a battering ram to break through walls, doors, and gates.

other attackers tried to climb over the walls with ladders. Defenders on the wall shoved the ladders away from the wall or pelted climbers with stones and arrows.

Another way that attackers reached the top of a wall was by using a wooden shelter on wheels, called a **siege tower**. Soldiers pushed the siege tower next to a curtain wall. A drawbridge at the tower's top allowed attacking soldiers to rush onto the battlements.

A siege tower had several levels. Men on the bottom level attacked the wall with picks or a battering ram. Middle levels

When attackers tried to climb over the walls, defenders pushed their ladders away and pelted them with rocks and arrows.

held archers who shot at the enemy on the wall. Several hundred men could fit inside the largest siege towers. For example, one used at Breteuil in France in 1356 had three stories, with each level holding three hundred men.

Defenders Resist

Defenders fought against the siege tower by pushing it over or throwing heavy rocks on it until it collapsed. They also tried to burn it, although attackers covered the siege tower with wet animal hides to resist flames.

If the castle was surrounded by water, the attacking army could not use its siege towers. But if the moat was dry, attackers filled the ditch with logs, brush, and dirt, then pushed the siege tower across to the castle wall.

Bombarding the Walls

Besides battering rams and siege towers, attackers used powerful throwing weapons to break into the castle. These weapons hurled rocks and boulders with enough force to weaken stone walls.

One of the most powerful and accurate throwing weapons was the **trebuchet**. Working like a combination of seesaw and slingshot, it could hurl 300-pound (136 kilogram) boulders at high speeds for hundreds of yards (meters).

Armies had special engineers to design trebuchets, siege towers, and battering rams. The large wooden machines were usually built at the scene of the siege, although sometimes they were made in advance and brought to the site in carts.

Bringing Down the Walls

Despite these special weapons, attackers were not always successful in breaking through or climbing the castle's walls. Another method they used was toppling the towers and curtain walls.

Attackers sometimes pushed a siege tower to the top of a curtain wall, and a drawbridge allowed soldiers to rush onto the battlement.

To bring down the walls, diggers called **sappers** tunneled underground until they reached the base of a tower or wall. They supported their tunnel with wood beams, then filled it with straw, brush, and animal fat. After crawling out of the tunnel, the sappers set fire to the brush. The flames burned the wooden supports, causing the tunnel to cave in and the stone wall above it to collapse.

Castle defenders did not always realize that sappers were at work. Even if they did know, they could only stop

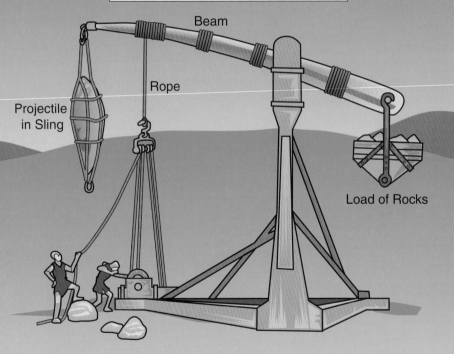

Operating a Trebuchet

Beam

Rope

Projectile in Sling

Load of Rocks

The trebuchet was operated using a load of rocks on the short end of the beam and a projectile held in a sling on the long end. When the rope holding the long end was released, the load of rocks dropped, swinging the beam forward and flinging the projectile.

them by digging into the tunnel from inside the castle and battling the sappers underground. The best way for defenders to prevent sapping was to build the castle on solid rock or to surround it with water.

The Siege of Rochester Castle

In 1215 England's King John used sappers to take control of Rochester Castle. After King John's soldiers broke down the castle's outer wall by bombarding it with rocks and chipping at its base with picks, the defenders retreated to the keep. Sappers dug a tunnel under a corner of the square-shaped keep, then set the tunnel on fire. Part of the keep collapsed, leading to the defenders' surrender.

Few castles could withstand a long siege and brutal assault. But assaults were dangerous and expensive for the attackers, too. As a result, most sieges ended with an agreement between defenders and attackers instead of a fight to the death.

The End of the Age of Castles

By the late fifteenth century, social and military changes brought the end of castle building. Skirmishes between rival nobles were less common. With the threat of attack and siege gone, wealthy landowners preferred to live in comfortable houses instead of drafty castles.

Cannons became powerful enough to destroy stone walls. Guns could shoot a hole in a wall or in a knight's armor. To defend against these weapons, castles needed major alterations. But by the end of the Middle Ages, the increased cost of hiring workers made construction expensive. Only a small number of nobles could afford to renovate an old castle or to build a new one.

With few new castles built and many older ones abandoned and crumbling into ruins, the age of castles was over.

Today stone castles left from the Middle Ages are used as homes, museums, and hotels.

Castles Today

Today the remaining stone castles are used as homes, museums, and hotels. In Britain, the earthen hills and ditches of one motte and bailey castle have even been turned into a golf course. Hundreds of years after medieval workers first built them, these structures from the age of castles survive.

Glossary

allegiance: Loyalty and service owed to a lord during medieval times.

archer: A soldier who shot arrows using a bow.

arrow loop: A slit in the castle wall through which arrows could be fired at attackers.

bailey: A courtyard inside the castle walls.

battering ram: A heavy wooden beam used to pound walls, gates, and doors until they broke.

battlement: A jagged top edge of a castle wall or tower that protected soldiers against attack.

Bayeux Tapestry: An eleventh-century wall hanging.

crenel: The open space in the battlement from which arrows could be shot or objects dropped.

curtain wall: The stone wall surrounding a castle.

drawbridge: A bridge that stretched across a moat and could be lifted to keep attackers out of the castle.

fortress: A strong building or group of buildings used for military defense.

garderobe: A toilet built into a castle wall.

gatehouse: A castle's fortified entrance that included towers, bridges, and other barriers.

hoarding: A wooden shelter built at the top of the outside edge of a castle wall to protect defenders as they shot arrows or dropped objects onto attackers below.

keep: A stone tower, which was often where the lord lived.

mason: A skilled stoneworker.

medieval: Referring to the Middle Ages.

merlon: The notched section of the battlement.

Middle Ages: The historical era from about A.D. 500 to 1500.

moat: A wide ditch, often filled with water, around a castle.

motte: A tall mound of dirt on which a tower was built.

murder holes: Openings in the gatehouse ceiling through which defenders shot arrows or dropped objects onto attackers.

nobles: Powerful landowners during the Middle Ages, including kings and barons.

palisade: A tall fence made from wooden stakes or logs.

portcullis: A wooden gate in the castle entrance.

sapper: An attacker who dug tunnels under a castle's walls in an attempt to make them collapse.

siege: An attack on a castle during which it was surrounded and sometimes bombarded until the defenders surrendered.

siege tower: A tall, wooden shelter used to move attackers next to a castle's walls.

trebuchet: A weapon used to hurl large objects at a castle.

wall walk: The area along the top of a castle wall from which defenders fought off attackers.

For Further Reading

Books

Malcolm Day, *The World of Castles and Forts*. New York: Peter Bedrick Books, 2001. This book uses colorful illustrations to show how castles and forts have changed throughout history.

Christopher Gravett, *Castle*. New York: Dorling Kindersley, 2000. Learn more about the building of castles, stone-working tools, weapons, and castle life.

Nicholas Harris and Peter Dennis (illustrator), *Fast Forward Castle*. Hauppauge, NY: Barron's Educational Services, 2001. Discover how a castle fortress in Europe changed from 600 B.C. to today. Full of detailed and entertaining illustrations.

David Macaulay, *Castle*. Boston: Houghton Mifflin, 1977. Using detailed drawings, this book follows the planning and construction of a castle in Wales in the thirteenth century.

Beth Smith, *Castles*. New York: Franklin Watts, 1988. Read about everyday castle life, siege warfare, and castle ghost stories.

Web Site

Castles of the World (www.castles.org). This site contains information about parts of a castle and includes the architectural plans for actual castles. Explore castles around the world through color photographs and videos. Check out the kids' section.

Internet Source

***NOVA*, "Medieval Siege: Secrets of Lost Empires,"** www.pbs.org. Find information about the attack and defense of a medieval castle. See a slide show about the building of a trebuchet. Design your own trebuchet and use it to play an online game called *Destroy the Castle*.

Index

arrow loops, 29–30
assaults, 33, 35–36, 38

baileys, 14, 16, 19
battering rams, 33, 35
battlements, 25
Bayeux Tapestry, 16
borders, 11
business, 8–9

cannons, 39
castles
    age of, 6, 39
    today, 40
chapels, 9
Chateau Gaillard, 31–32
clearings, 26
conditions, 9
construction
    of motte and bailey castles,
        14–16
    of stone castles, 19–22
cost, 11
crenels, 25
curtain walls, 19, 24

defenses
    assaults and, 33, 35–36, 38
    locations and, 12–13
    sieges and, 23, 32–33

of stone castles, 18–19,
    24–26, 28–30
trickery and, 31–32
of wooden castles, 15–16
doors, 30
drawbridges, 16, 28–29

garderobes, 10
gatehouses, 16, 26, 28
government, 8
great halls, 9

hedges, 26
hoardings, 25–26

John (king of England), 39

keeps
    design change of, 29
    of stone castles, 18–19
    of wooden castles, 15–16
kings, 6, 11
knights, 8

land, 6,–11
living quarters
    comforts in, 9–10
    design change of, 29
    of stone castles, 18–19
    of wooden castles, 15–16

locations, 11–13

masons, 20
materials, 14–16, 18–22
merlons, 25
Middle Ages, 6
moats, 15, 16, 26
motte and bailey castles,
    14–16, 18
murder holes, 29

name, 11
nobles, 6, 8

palisades, 16
peasants, 8
porticullis, 28–29
purposes, 6, 8–9, 10–12

Richard the Lion-Hearted
(king of England), 31
Rochester Castle, 39

sappers, 36, 38–39
sieges, 23, 32–33
siege towers, 35–36
sites, 11–13

toilets, 10
towers, 29–30
trebuchet, 36
trickery, 31–32
tunneling, 36, 38–39

wall walks, 19
warfare, 11
    see also defenses
wooden castles, 14–16, 18

Picture Credits

Cover image: Corel
© Paul Almasy/CORBIS, 25
© Archivo Iconografico, S.A./CORBIS, 35
© Stephanie Colasanti/CORBIS, 40
Corel, 12, 22
S.V. Crognan/Art Resource, NY, 24
© James Davis; Eye Ubiquitous/CORBIS, 20
Giraudon/Art Resource, NY, 21
Chris Jouan, 15, 18
Erich Lessing/Art Resource, NY, 32, 34
© Massimo Listri/CORBIS, 10
© North Wind Picture Archives, 8, 37
Photodisc, 7, 12 (inset)
© Christian Sarramon/CORBIS, 27
Snark/Art Resource, NY, 17

About the Author

Gail Jarrow is the author of nonfiction books, novels, and magazine articles for young readers. Before becoming an author, she taught science and math in elementary and middle schools. Jarrow received her undergraduate degree in zoology from Duke University and her master's degree from Dartmouth College. She has visited several medieval castles in Europe.